INDIGENOUS HISTORY FROM 1961–1977

THE CIVIL RIGHTS ERA

by E. A. Hale

WWW.FOCUSREADERS.COM

Copyright © 2025 by Focus Readers®, Mendota Heights, MN 55120. All rights reserved. No part of this book may be reproduced or utilized in any form or by any means without written permission from the publisher.

Focus Readers is distributed by North Star Editions:
sales@northstareditions.com | 888-417-0195

Produced for Focus Readers by Red Line Editorial.

Content Consultant: Katrina Phillips, PhD, Red Cliff Band of Lake Superior Ojibwe, Associate Professor of History, Macalester College

Photographs ©: BB/AP Images, cover, 1; F. Peter Weil/NAES College Collection, 4–5; Bettmann/Getty Images, 7, 15; Jack Vartoogian/Archive Photos/Getty Images, 9; Lui Kit Wong/The News Tribune/AP Images, 11; David Pollack/Corbis Historical/Getty Images, 12–13; AP Images, 17, 23; National Archives, 18–19; Red Line Editorial, 21; Foc Kan/WireImage/Getty Images, 24–25; Kathy Willens/AP Images, 27; Pictorial Parade/Keystone/Archive Photos/Getty Images, 29

Library of Congress Cataloging-in-Publication Data
Library of Congress Cataloging-in-Publication Data is available on the Library of Congress website.

ISBN
979-8-88998-415-3 (hardcover)
979-8-88998-443-6 (paperback)
979-8-88998-495-5 (ebook pdf)
979-8-88998-471-9 (hosted ebook)

Printed in the United States of America
Mankato, MN
012025

ABOUT THE TERMINOLOGY

The terms **American Indians** and **Native Americans** are used interchangeably throughout this book. With more than 570 federally recognized tribes or nations in the United States, the usage will vary. Native nations and their people may use either term. The term **Indigenous peoples** describes groups of people who have lived in an area since prehistory. It may also be used as a shorter term to describe the federal designation **American Indians**, **Alaska Natives**, and **Native Hawaiians**.

ABOUT THE AUTHOR

E. A. Hale is a proud member of the Choctaw Nation of Oklahoma.

TABLE OF CONTENTS

CHAPTER 1

Protests 5

VOICES FROM THE PAST

Ramona Bennett 10

CHAPTER 2

Sovereignty Rising 13

CHAPTER 3

Push and Pull 19

CHAPTER 4

Benefits of Activism 25

Focus Questions • 30
Glossary • 31
To Learn More • 32
Index • 32

CHAPTER 1

PROTESTS

The **civil rights** era was about righting the wrongs of the past. People forced laws to change. Many of the old laws had targeted minorities, such as Native people. In 1961, the National Congress of American Indians (NCAI) met in Chicago, Illinois. This group worked for Native **self-determination**. The event

Five hundred Native Americans attended the 1961 NCAI conference. They were part of 90 tribes and bands.

encouraged Native people to advocate for their nations.

Indigenous people stood up for their rights. This included fighting for their hunting and fishing rights. In Washington State, this struggle became known as the

MENOMINEE TRIBE V. UNITED STATES

In 1968, the Wisconsin Menominee tribe sued the United States. The tribe argued for its rights to hunt and fish. These rights came from the **Treaty of Wolf River in 1854**. In 1968, the US Supreme Court agreed with the Menominee. The ruling applied to all US tribes. All Native nations would have their rights to hunt and fish. Congress could not cancel a treaty unless it passed a new law.

Indigenous people take part in a fish-in on the Nisqually River in 1966.

Fish Wars. Native people in the Pacific Northwest had always fished for salmon. The US government had promised this right in a treaty. But in 1963, game wardens began arresting Native people for fishing. Native people kept fishing. They held a protest similar to a **sit-in**. But it was a "fish-in" on the river. They were fined and jailed again and again. But Native people kept their traditions alive.

Native people also claimed their water and land rights. Some wanted to save their lakes and rivers. Tribes pushed for the return of their homelands. The US government had sold most of the land. So, the tribes demanded the return of unused lands. Some also took over lands that were owned by the government.

Native people also tried to save their cultures. For example, in Hawai'i, they rallied to save their language and arts. They held protests to save their sacred sites. The US government was using these lands for roads and the military.

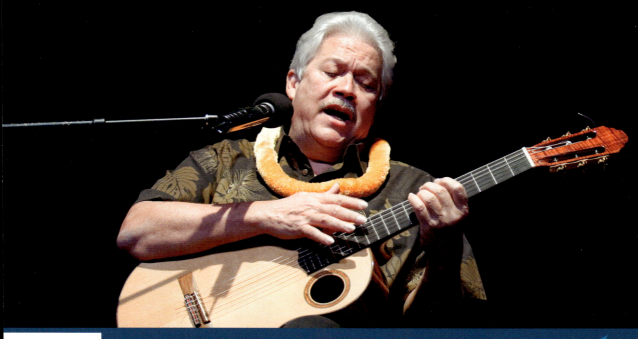

Native Hawaiians worked to protect their arts, such as music, dance, and healing.

In 1970, the US government set up the Community Health Medic Program. Some Indigenous veterans had served as medics in the Vietnam War (1954–1975). The program helped them find jobs back home. Veterans could use their medical skills from the military to help people on remote **reservations** in the United States.

> **VOICES FROM THE PAST**

RAMONA BENNETT

Ramona Bennett of the Puyallup Tribe was a civil rights **activist**. She was jailed for her actions. For example, she took part in a fish-in on the Puyallup River near Tacoma, Washington, in 1970. Bennett had a small typewriter. She had a little tape player to record sounds, too. She wrote news reports for radio and TV stations. Bennett said, "We were very, very visible. We got TVs and lined them up."[1] Soon, the fish-in made headlines.

The Puyallup also fought for their land. The government had promised to build a hospital for the Puyallup. But the US government closed the hospital in 1959. They gave the building to the state of Washington. In 1976, Bennett and other Puyallup people took over the building. They hung out a long banner in protest. It could be seen from

Ramona Bennett stands in front of the building she helped take over in 1976.

the freeway. The public supported the tribe. There were peace talks with the state. This event led to a big settlement for the tribe. The state paid the tribe for land the United States had taken. The tribe also won back the right to fish.

1. "The Fish Wars: Strategies for Taking Action." *Native Knowledge 360°*. National Museum of the American Indian, n.d. Web. 10 June 2024.

CHAPTER 2

SOVEREIGNTY RISING

By the end of the 1960s, most US **termination** policies had ended. But these laws had already harmed Native nations. During the termination era, the United States had passed 60 laws and policies that aimed to break up tribes. Native nations lost millions of acres of tribal land.

> Native activism helped end termination. This allowed Native nations to make more decisions for themselves.

In response, many Native groups worked for their land rights. For instance, small groups of Alaska Natives had lobbied for land rights for years. Then they came together to form the Alaska Federation of Natives in 1966. The group said its people had always owned the land. But the state had taken it. In 1971, Congress listened. The US government returned millions of acres to Alaska Natives. The state paid Native companies for the rest of the land.

Policies like relocation had also pushed many Indigenous people to cities. New Native groups formed in response. Ojibwe and Dakota people in Minneapolis,

Ojibwe activist Dennis Banks helped start the American Indian Movement (AIM). AIM pushed for the rights of all Natives.

Minnesota, created the American Indian Movement (AIM) in 1968. They worked to support Native people in the city. The group staged protests. It helped those who spoke out for fairness. AIM fought for

15

justice. In some cases, the group clashed with police.

Alcatraz Island served as another place for Native protests. This island is in San Francisco Bay. Indigenous people had

INDIAN CIVIL RIGHTS ACT

Sovereign Native nations existed before the United States existed. Tribes did not write the US Constitution. This document protects civil rights. Tribes are not bound by it. For this reason, Congress passed the Indian Civil Rights Act in 1968. It said Native nations must protect civil rights. But the act took some power away from tribes when deciding civil rights issues. It gave some power to US courts. Even so, a Native nation makes its own rules. For example, it may decide its tribe's religion. US governments cannot.

Indigenous activists lived on Alcatraz Island for 19 months. The site was a symbol of Native activism.

used the island long before the United States claimed it. In 1969, American Indians took over the empty prison on the island. They claimed the island for all American Indians. They wrote, "We hold the rock!" They also wanted to build a cultural center.

CHAPTER 3

PUSH AND PULL

In 1970, the US president spoke to Congress. He called on lawmakers to reverse the policies of termination. This would let Native nations self-determine, or decide, their own futures. It would protect tribes and their citizens.

Congress passed the Indian Education Act in 1972. It set up funds to help all

The US government took Taos Pueblo homeland in 1906. In 1970, Taos Pueblo people won back much of their land.

Native students. The law gave money to form parent groups. Parents served as school advisors. They helped schools teach Native cultures in classrooms.

Native activists kept pushing for more changes. Activists drove from the West Coast to Washington, DC, in 1972. They called it the Trail of Broken Treaties. Seven hundred people from more than 200 tribes took part. They took over the government-run Bureau of Indian Affairs (BIA) building for a whole week. This sit-in shed light on ways US laws had failed Native people.

In 1973, about 200 Oglala Lakota people asked AIM for help. They were tired of being targeted by their own corrupt tribal government. Together, they took over a trading post on the Wounded Knee site. Wounded Knee is a historic

THE TRAIL OF BROKEN TREATIES

Three caravans started on the West Coast and joined in Minnesota. A fourth caravan started in Eastern Oklahoma. All met in Washington, DC.

place in South Dakota. In one day in 1890, US soldiers had killed hundreds of Native people there.

Like before, the 1973 standoff turned deadly. Two American Indians died, and others were hurt. Even so, the public heard their stories. Many people rallied for Native rights.

Native activism pushed Congress to do more. In 1974, Congress passed the Native American Programs Act. It helped fight poverty. The purpose was to promote well-being for all Native people. The act set up an office to help Native Americans. It offered job training. Native people could earn better wages.

Bobby Onco of the Kiowa nation celebrates at the end of the 1973 Occupation of Wounded Knee.

In 1975, Congress finally recognized that Native self-determination mattered. It passed the Indian Self-Determination and Education Assistance Act. The law let tribes make their own decisions. It allowed tribes to manage their own schools, too. Tribes knew how to best serve their own people.

CHAPTER 4

BENEFITS OF ACTIVISM

Indigenous people held many protests during the civil rights era. They went from coast to coast. Activists came from tribes all over the country. They spoke with one strong voice. They used **civil disobedience** to show their outrage. Their actions let the public know how past laws had hurt Natives. Government laws had

Madonna Thunder Hawk helped form Women of All Red Nations (WARN) in 1974. WARN focused on Native women's rights.

harmed tribal sovereignty. Change was needed for Native people of all tribes.

Over time, their activism stopped the US policies of termination. Their actions moved the policies toward self-determination for tribes. New laws protected sovereign nations. Native

LITTLE EARTH

In 1973, Little Earth was built in Minneapolis. The apartments can house more than 200 Indigenous families. They meet the need for low-rent housing in the city. Little Earth was the first government housing project that rented mostly to Indigenous people. Those who lived there came from many tribes. AIM helped with the project. Little Earth still serves Native people today.

Betty Mae Jumper was the first female leader of the Seminole Tribe of Florida. She helped improve health care for the Seminoles.

people were able to revive cultural practices.

In 1976, Congress passed the Indian Health Care Improvement Act. It helped pay for health care for all Native people. Many lived in remote places across the country. It helped pay for their training in the field of health. The act also helped build and improve clinics.

Despite new laws, some Native people were not happy with the US government. One reason was the BIA. Indigenous activists wanted the BIA to be shut down. They claimed it did not help them. They said the BIA often made policies without input from Native nations.

So, Native people protested with the Trail of Self-Determination. This 1976 rally was similar to the 1972 Trail of Broken Treaties. Like before, activists drove from the West Coast to Washington, DC. Protesters joined forces in front of the BIA office. But unlike

The 1976 Trail of Self-Determination helped continue Indigenous activism to the present day.

before, they were not allowed into the BIA building. Still, people rallied for Native rights. They held traditional events in the capital. They beat drums. They chanted. The rally was shown on the news. It got more support from the public. Indigenous people continued pushing for change.

FOCUS QUESTIONS

Write your answers on a separate piece of paper.

1. Indigenous people protested during the civil rights era. What were some of their reasons?

2. Why do you think activists from many Native nations came together for protests?

3. Where was the site of two standoffs (one in 1890 and one in 1973) between Native Americans and the US government?
    - **A.** Alcatraz Island
    - **B.** Washington, DC
    - **C.** Wounded Knee

4. Activism by Indigenous people resulted in which of the following?
    - **A.** new laws that ended Native sovereignty
    - **B.** new laws that protected Native sovereignty
    - **C.** less government aid being given to tribes

Answer key on page 32.

GLOSSARY

activist
A person who takes action to make social or political changes.

civil disobedience
A protest in which people disobey laws they find unjust.

civil rights
Rights that protect people's freedom and equality.

reservations
Land set aside by the US government for Native nations.

self-determination
The ability for Native nations to decide what is best for tribal citizens.

sit-in
A protest in which people refuse to leave a place.

sovereign
Having the power to make rules and decisions without being controlled by another country.

termination
The process of ending a Native nation's status as a federally recognized tribe.

treaty
A binding agreement between the US government and a Native nation made before 1871.

TO LEARN MORE

BOOKS

Lindstrom, Carole. *We Are Water Protectors*. New York: Roaring Brook Press, 2020.

McDonald, Liam. *Indigenous America*. New York: Penguin Workshop, 2022.

Sorell, Traci. *We Are Still Here! Native American Truths Everyone Should Know*. Watertown, MA: Charlesbridge Publishing, 2021.

NOTE TO EDUCATORS

Visit **www.focusreaders.com** to find lesson plans, activities, links, and other resources related to this title.

INDEX

Alaska Natives, 14
Alcatraz Island, 16–17
American Indian Movement (AIM), 15–16, 20–21, 26

Bennett, Ramona, 10
Bureau of Indian Affairs (BIA), 20, 28–29

Dakota people, 14

Fish Wars, 6–7

Hawai'i, 8

Menominee tribe, 6

National Congress of American Indians (NCAI), 6

Oglala Lakota people, 20–21
Ojibwe people, 14

Pacific Northwest, 7
Puyallup Tribe, 10–11

Trail of Broken Treaties, 20–21, 28
Trail of Self-Determination, 28

Vietnam War, 9

Wounded Knee, 20–22

Answer Key: 1. Answers will vary; 2. Answers will vary; 3. C; 4. B